Contents

CW01652648

'Teach by doing whenever you can. . . .' Jean-Jacque Rousseau

ACKNOWLEDGEMENTS

The author wishes to thank the following:
P. G. Carter, ML Biol, Director of the Countryside Education Trust, for major contributions to the sections dealing with project work in gardens and on estates at historic houses.
R. E. Thornbury, Warden of Sherbrooke Teachers Centre, Inner London Education Authority, for general advice upon suitable topics for specific age-groups and especially for the checklist on page 30.

Produced and published by Heritage Books, 86 Brancaster Lane, Purley, Surrey
Designed by Fetherstonhaugh Associates, London
Printed by Robert MacLehose & Co. Ltd, Glasgow

The Heritage: An Introduction

Chapter One

LEARNING BY DOING

Four authorities in Great Britain own, or have custody of, more than eight hundred properties of great historical interest. They are, of course, the National Trust, the National Trust for Scotland, the Department of the Environment and the Historic Houses Association. For many years schools have been visiting these properties, especially castles, and have been using their visits as the basis for history projects. The opportunities for projects at historic houses are, however, less familiar because far fewer visits have been made to them by schools.

In order to correct this discrepancy, a national scheme was launched by the Historic Houses Association in March 1977 under the title 'Heritage Education Year', the declared purpose of which was ' . . . to make everyone, owners, teachers, parents and children more aware of the exciting educational potential of historic buildings, their contents and estates'. As a direct result of this initiative, owners and custodians have become far more aware of the needs of schools visiting their properties and many are now developing curricula materials of great educational value. Such aids as worksheets based upon the contents of their houses, family museums, or nearby churches; leaflets on woodland or riverside walks; and collections of items for children to handle, are already available at many properties. The purpose of this book is to suggest to teachers how these valuable new facilities may be set to educational advantage and it is hoped that owners and custodians of properties will find it equally useful as a guide to what teachers will need during their visits with groups of children. To make it possible, in short, for children to learn by doing when they visit the historic houses which are their heritage.

A HOUSE IS A HOUSE

A family house, lived in by passing generations, is captive history. The smallest cottage, if it happens to have been the home of Shakespeare's mother-in-law, will attract the homage of millions. The greatest palace, too vast for family life, can still have a corner—Winston Churchill's birth room at Blenheim—where the human scale persists. Family homes, historic palaces, rustic cottages, they all speak to us about the past. But for children, the only voices heard are those of people—the builders, owners, servants, of once-upon-a-time.

PEOPLE ARE EVERYTHING

To the practical minds of children, therefore, the fabric of an old house is only relevant as a backcloth to real life. Inigo Jones or Vanbrugh may have shaped its towers and collonades; the brothers Adam may have added exquisite detail; Grinling Gibbons himself may have carved miracles, but children will wonder less about the gilding and the subtle curves than about the artists and craftsmen who created them and the men and women for whom they worked.

'How long did it take to carve that lot?' 'How much did he charge for it?' 'How could anybody have been rich enough to buy a house like this?' 'Why have *all* those people in that row of portraits got big noses?' Those are the questions of childhood for they stem from the only base from which children can judge history—the present. They are excellent questions, the very stuff of teaching and once they have been answered and the people brought to life, children can be led to more thoughtful things. They can be introduced to the aesthetics of the houses; the elegance and beauty which craftsmen and owners worked to achieve. For that is what makes Britain's heritage of country houses unique. There is not an ugly one amongst them.

THE PROJECT METHOD

The prime advantage of the method of teaching by projects is, of course, the opportunity it affords for the integration of subjects in the curriculum. It provides reasons for creative writing, art, science, history, geography and craft. It also offers teachers opportunities for organising group work and individual studies within groups. A well-planned project (which means enough time left for its successful completion!), can give shape to a term's work and, by means of a classroom display for 'open day', provide practical evidence of work well done.

The choice of subject for a project is therefore crucial. Make it too narrow—for example 'Railways' and there would not be scope for all the ancillary subjects needed to balance the curriculum; make it too open-ended—for example 'Civilisation', and three years of group work could not do justice to the theme. In the context of the historic house we have suggested in every case subjects for projects which will give adequate scope whilst limiting the subject matter to that which could be reasonably encompassed by, say, six groups of five children in a class of thirty, working for the equivalent of one day a week on the project for a term, with perhaps a little additional work at home.

The most important factor of all is planning. It is also arguably the most useful educationally for as R. L. Stevenson said so well, 'To travel hopefully is a better thing than to arrive and the true success is to labour'. The final accomplishment of a project is of little importance as compared with the labour on the way, and of the labour, the planning stage is the most valuable–and pleasurable.

This book deals specifically with the opportunities for project work at the hundreds of splendid historic houses which are our heritage and which, through the stimulus of Heritage Education Year, are now welcoming school visits for this purpose. The actual visit, however, can only represent a small fraction of the total time spent on the project. It is therefore doubly important that the visit is carefully planned to make the best of what time is available.

PLANNING A VISIT

Owners and custodians of historic houses are, of course, anxious that schools should make the best use possible of their visits. They are happy to discuss plans with teachers in advance of their visit and for this purpose teachers are advised to make an exploratory call at the house they have chosen for their project at least three weeks before the planned date. This can be arranged by letter or phone and, normally, no charge will be made for entry on this occasion. Teachers are advised to read as much as possible about the house before they make their planning visit and the local library will often provide useful references, sometimes even privately published histories of the house itself written by proud owners in the past. Much can be planned in advance and confirmed by this first visit and, knowing the general requirement, owners will often take a personal interest and make available relevant things for the children to see which will help them with their project on 'the day'. If they are available, teachers should buy a range of slides, photographs, postcards, worksheets, etc., at the house.

After this advance visit, teachers may feel reluctant to tell their children too much about the house in case they spoil it for them by making everything too familiar. Children, however, like to recognise the familiar, and indeed find great difficulty in making sense of the unfamiliar. They should be shown as many photographs as possible and supplied with as much descriptive material as can be found. Get as much of the project work done as possible before the visit and use the visit to correct errors. There will then be excited cries of: 'That is the room where so and so was locked up!' instead of a dull: 'Wonder what that place was for.'

The division of work within a class can sometimes be a problem. Jane Snooks is good at art–should she therefore lead a group producing a collage picture of the house? Patrick Snooks is very keen on making models–should he be part of the team making a model of the farm buildings? If either Snooks is in need of a success to boost morale, then the answer is yes. If that is not important, then the answer is probably no; expand their experience by letting them try something they find difficult with a promise of 'a go' at their forte if they do well. Shared work, however, must be the essence of projects with an opportunity for the exercise of leadership for individuals within each group–an opportunity teachers should not miss.

HOW OWNERS AND CUSTODIANS WILL HELP

If they know details of the plan well in advance, owners and custodians will generally help in many ways to make the school visit a success. Some owners or custodians will be ready to give children a brief talk about some aspect of their property which is relevant to the project; many are now providing rooms where children can work during their visit and there may be items available for children to handle and examine. Interesting books or documents may also be open for inspection for children to take written extracts.

Teachers will, of course, be aware of the need for children to understand that the contents of the historic houses they visit are very valuable, often irreplaceable. Planning for the visit should include an explanation of this aspect so that the children behave sensibly and take care not to cause damage. It is especially important that children realise that there will be other visitors besides themselves and that they must take care not to spoil the day for others by less than best behaviour. A well-worked-out plan will, of course, keep them so busy and interested that warnings of this kind will not be necessary.

AND THE NEXT VISIT

An historic house near a school can become a permanently available teaching asset. Teachers for their own interest–from which must stem the interest of their pupils–will wish to select new topics for subsequent visits. It is sensible, therefore, to build up a working background with reserves of materials, by keeping postcards, worksheets and photographs for future return visits. This is especially important if the house concerned does not itself provide educational materials.

Chapter Two

The House: Upstairs and Belowstairs

The interest which children can generate in an historic house must be directly related to their own experience, and in school parties there will be children from tower blocks, 'semi's', farms and children's homes. Age will also limit the awareness which promotes imagination. Starting points must therefore be graded in degrees of difficulty and the suggestions which follow are arranged with this in mind. The questionnaires are given in detail for the house-owner to anticipate the questions likely to be asked about his house, and for the teacher to explore when making a preparatory visit and to use as the basis for the planning phase described in Chapter One.

Several activities are suggested under each project so that teachers can organise their classes into working groups in advance of the visit. Not all of the questions can necessarily be answered by the owner of the house. Many will have to be the subject of library visits before or after the visit to the historic house. Pattern the day so that too much time is not spent indoors. Leave time for visits to outbuildings, gardens and the estate.

SUGGESTED PROJECT 1: CHILDREN OF THE HOUSE

Research

Is there a family portrait depicting children of school age? Who were they and where was the portrait painted? What sort of clothes did they wear? Did they go to school and if so, where? If not, did they have a tutor, and which was the schoolroom? What games did they play and where in the house? Are any of their toys still to be seen? What did they do when it rained and they could not go out? Are there samplers done by the girls? Any models made by the boys? Where did they sleep, wash, eat? Is there a story connected with a child of the house which could be the subject of a play or piece of writing?

Activities

Writing: Tell a story about a day in the life of one of the children of the house.

Mathematics: Work out how many children have lived in the house since it was built.

Art: Draw and paint a picture about some of them.

Craft: Sew a doll's dress like that worn by one of the girls who lived in the house. Make a peepshow in a cardboard box of one of the rooms in the house with the children playing.

SUGGESTED PROJECT 2: A CHRISTMAS OR BIRTHDAY PARTY

Research

Imagine that you are one of the children in the picture. You have to help arrange a Christmas/birthday party. Where would you hold it? How many guests could you have (count the chairs)? What would you have to eat (remember how long ago you lived)? Where would it be cooked and by whom? Who would serve the food; who would wash up afterwards? If you wanted to dance, how would the music be made? How would your guests travel to the house? Pretend that it was a very snowy Christmas/birthday. How would the house be kept warm? How would it be lit? What clothes would your friends have worn for the party?

Activities

Writing: Write a story about the day of the party. Make something exciting happen.

Mathematics: Work out how much the party would have cost.

Art: Draw and paint a picture about everybody enjoying the party.

Craft: Invite your best doll to the party and make a special dress for her like one of the dresses in the picture. Make a model in a cardboard box of the kitchen with the cook making the food for the party.

SUGGESTED PROJECT 3: A REAL-LIFE DRAMA

Research

If there is an historic figure connected with the house about whom a story can be told the house can be used as the setting for a play to be written and acted by the children. A female character is desirable because historic houses tend to be rather male-orientated (suits of armour, weapons, etc.). If the house-owner can provide information about a suitable character, the project could then be planned as follows:

Activities

Writing: Write a play about the famous character. Include as many characters in addition as possible so that most of the class can take part.

Art: Make scenery for the play.

Craft: Make swords, helmets, dresses, etc., for the play.

Music: Record (or better still, play) music of the period to accompany the acting. (If you ask, the owner of the house may let you act the play in the place where it actually happened.)

SUGGESTED PROJECT 4: THE LIVING HOUSE

Research

Houses grow—or shrink—to suit the needs of their occupiers. In modern times, carports are added, lofts are converted to bedrooms and prefabricated sun rooms are tacked on to sitting rooms. It is an historic process and most historic houses have been changed in this way. The changes tell much about the families themselves—houses grow to match affluence and increase in numbers; they shrink to meet falling income or change in family size. Alterations also reflect changes in fashion and improvements in hygiene and standards of comfort. A project based on this theme can explore every aspect of social life as well as investigating the techniques and economics of house building.

Activities

Writing: 1. Make a family tree showing the people who lived in the house from the time it was built until modern times. Mark the dates when changes were made to the house.
2. Try to find, by research, what some of the alterations to the house cost. Write letters from the owners to builders telling them what to do.
3. Pretend you are the house. Tell the story of how you were changed through the years and why.
Mathematics: Try to find out how much one of the building changes cost or how much the original building cost. Compare it with the cost today. Take a pocket calculator with you to count brickwork, etc.
Art: Make drawings showing the house at various times in its construction and later development.
Craft: Make models of the house showing the changes which took place.

SUGGESTED PROJECT 5: THE HOUSE AND THE VILLAGE

Research

Great houses have traditionally provided the main source of livelihood for their nearby villages. They have often owned them. The manorial system was, of course, the prime example of this social organisation. It still applies in modified form just as the row of suburban shops caters for the needs of its immediate rows of 'semi's'. The staff of the great house was drawn largely from local people as were the estate workers. A project on this theme can be brought right up to date.

Activities

Writing: Make a chart to show the staff of the house at the height of its prosperity. Make a list of the individuals on the staff and describe what each one did. See if you can find out the names of some of them. If they came from the nearby village see if there are still families with those names living in the village.

Mathematics: Find out how much each member of the staff was paid. What was the total cost of running the household? How much would it cost today?

Art: Find out what clothes were worn by some of the servants—livery for the footmen and coachmen, smocks for the outdoor workers, etc. Make drawings to show what they were like.

Craft: Make a model of the outside of the house. Use Airfix people to stand in front of it to represent the staff who ran the house. Make a model of inside the house.

SUGGESTED PROJECT 6: THE VILLAGE

Research

The house may have developed educational materials for nature or woodland trails as well as worksheets based on the local church, family museum, etc., or for a village survey. These should be investigated during the preliminary visit and modified for use with the projects chosen. Activities possible in a village are, of course, too varied to be encapsulated under one heading but some relevant questions in a village survey could be: How far do people have to go to get groceries, a haircut, dental treatment? Is there a common or green, a glebe farm, a church with banners or manorial coats of arms, etc.? Is there a school? How old is it? How many children are taught there? Is there a war memorial? What rights of way are there across the fields?—trace their routes on a map and find out why they were first established.

Tape recordings can be made of the stories of older people in the village. These should be kept for future visits so as not to keep bothering people.

Chapter Three

The Outbuildings

The outbuildings to great houses were often as beautiful in their construction and design as the house itself. At first, almost every domestic function concerned with service to the family was banished outside but later they were absorbed into the main structure, often into ill-lit and badly ventilated basements.

At the height of their prosperity many of the great houses were self-sufficient for every need from brewing to flour milling and the work of the blacksmith. Evidence of these activities has now been mostly swept away but many houses still retain the equipment of the brewhouse, the dairy, the stables and, of course, the carriage and harness rooms. Here ancient crafts were carried on and new crafts–for example, motor car servicing–learned. There was a sporting and recreational aspect too: falconry, the dovecot, hunt kennels and the gamekeeper's store. Evidence of many of these activities may still be found in the outbuildings of some historic houses.

SUGGESTED PROJECT 1: THE STABLES

Research

How many horses did the household need for various purposes–travel, sport, work? How were the horses looked after and by whom? What crafts were involved in the care of horses? What were the advantages of horses for the various purposes of the household and what were the disadvantages as compared with modern machines? Why have machines taken over from horses?

Activities

Writing: 1. Write a story about a day in the life of one of the horses that served the people of the house.

2. Imagine you were the first owner of the house. You have to give instructions to the builder for stables to be built. Write a letter to him explaining exactly what will be required.

Art: Make a series of pictures showing the various activities concerned with horses–grooming, shoeing, harnessing and saddling-up, exercising them.

Craft: Make a model of a block of stables.

SUGGESTED PROJECT 2: THE COACH HOUSE OR GARAGE

Research

How many vehicles did the house need at the height of its prosperity? What were they for? If there are coaches or carriages left from the days of horses, study them and find out: how they were steered, how they were sprung, how the wheels were made, how the body was fitted to the chassis. How far could carriages travel without changing horses? How did the posting system work? How many people were employed to care for and drive the carriages?

Activities

Writing: 1. Describe a day in the life of a coachman. Make the story exciting. Perhaps the coach could be stopped by highwaymen or have an accident.

2. Give written orders to a coachbuilder for a new coach. Explain exactly how you want it to be and full details of its colour, upholstery, etc. Write the reply from the coachbuilder and give his bill for the work.

Art: Make accurate drawings of a coach, or carriage showing how they were built.

Craft: Make a model of a coach or carriage.

SUGGESTED PROJECT 3: SPORTS AND GAMES

Research

How did the people of the house amuse themselves? What games did they play? Hunting, fishing and shooting were the three traditional country hobbies. What outbuildings were needed for all these activities? Perhaps they once kept falcons or practised archery.

Activities

The opportunities for projects based upon this subject are not likely to be as formalised as, for example, the transportation arrangements needed by the house. Activities are therefore less easy to suggest in advance. Obvious activities would be the study of falconry or archery, both of which have fascinating histories and offer many opportunities for written work and art.

Craft work connected with this project is less easy to suggest.

SUGGESTED PROJECT 4: THE FAMILY CHURCH OR CHAPEL

Research

If there is a family church or chapel, there will almost certainly be scope for investigations into the family history. Brass rubbings may be possible (this should be investigated at the preliminary visit so that materials can be taken). How old is the oldest tomb and the newest? What was the historical background of each? Are there famous names there—crusaders, merchants, civil war victims, First or Second World War casualties? It may be possible, albeit a little gloomy on a bright summer day, to locate the tombs of some whose portraits are in the house.

Activities

Writing: 1. Write a sermon to be delivered on Christmas Eve at a significantly historical time in the past.
2. Imagine one of the figures on a tomb comes to life and joins a modern school party visiting the church or chapel. Write an account of the conversation which ensues.
3. Research and describe a family wedding.
Art: Draw some of the details in the church—wood or stone carvings, angels, or gargoyles. Make a drawing of the church or chapel from the outside.
Craft: Make brass rubbings if this can be arranged. Make a model of the church tower with a bell in it.

The Gardens

Chapter Four

The gardens of most historic houses were laid out, in the first instance, for pleasure alone. The collection of rare plants, their classification, and arrangement of the gardens to provide suitable habitats, this mostly came later. There is thus room in most gardens for both aesthetics and botany. The more practical aspects of domestic economy can be studied in the kitchen garden and the herb garden can lead to both culinary and curative investigations.

It is important to establish during the preparatory visit whether specimens of leaves, flowers, etc., may be collected and it is as well to solicit the assistance and approval of gardeners if a project is to be undertaken.

SUGGESTED PROJECT 1: A PLEASURE GARDEN

Research

Gardens are arranged round houses to give pleasure like a picture. They can be works of real art. Usually they are arranged, first to give pleasure when seen from the house, and second to be beautiful to walk in. How was this managed by the designer of this garden? Are there terraces, avenues of trees, rose, water or rock gardens? Is there a lake or a fishpond? Summer houses or grottoes? Is there a gazebo or ha-ha? Are there specially arranged views? Does the garden improve the setting of the house?

Activities

Writing: Pretend you are the owner of the great house. Write to a garden designer telling him that you would like to have an area of land close to the house made into a garden.

Write the reply from the designer giving his plan for the layout with details of the work involved.

Mathematics: Find out the cost of the materials needed to make the garden as it is planned. Work out the total cost of the garden.

Art: Make a plan of the garden and give an artist's impression of what it will look like.

Craft: Make a model of the planned garden (see model-making chapter, page 27).

SUGGESTED PROJECT 2: PATTERNS AND SYMMETRY

Research

Study the leaves and flowers of plants to find examples of radial and bi-lateral symmetry. Find also interesting asymmetrical shapes. Some leaves from trees will provide good examples. Find very large leaves and compare them with very small ones. Most flowers are beautiful; some are ugly. Find examples of each and establish why they differ aesthetically.

Activities

Writing: Write copy for a poster advertising the gardens to the public.
Art: Make sketches of plants, flowers and leaves while in the gardens and use them in designing the poster.
Craft: Make artificial flowers by some of the many very well established techniques using crepe-paper, felt, Plasticine, etc.

SUGGESTED PROJECT 3: NATURAL HABITATS

Research

Explore the garden and discover what different habitats have been created for the various kinds of plants—sun-loving, shade-loving, water plants, marsh plants, alpine plants, etc. Notice the ways in which they grow to obtain the best advantage of their sites. It will be noticed that differences of habitat exist, for example, within a rock garden and in or near water and that plants have specialised habits which suit each.

Activities

Writing: Make lists of plants which love and hate sunshine; like and dislike lime; need heat or can do without it. Relate these characteristics to geographical areas.
Art: Draw and paint a chart showing where the main divisions of plants live—tropical rain forest, alpine, desert areas, etc.
Practical: Make a garden in the classroom. Shallow plastic seed trays, a bag of seed compost and another of potting compost will provide the basis. Let children decide, within reasonable limits, what they would like to grow. Good subjects are cacti and succulents (the 'Busy Lizzies' are good tempered). Miniature alpine gardens in window boxes outside are attractive and small plastic containers holding water can be used to create temporary gardens with moss, gravel and fronds of fern or duckweed. See also the technique described in the model-making chapter, page 26.

SUGGESTED PROJECT 4: THE PLEASURES OF A GARDEN

Research

Much has been written, poetry and prose, in praise of gardens. Classroom study of some of this written work can be related to a real garden (weather very much permitting) and the descriptions of poets and authors compared with reality. If owners of houses or their gardeners are willing to co-operate, the pleasures of a garden can be greatly enhanced by allowing children to enjoy the environment with more than one sense. If they close their eyes can they hear the garden? Do different parts of the garden 'sound' different? Will the gardeners allow them to touch some of the plants? Can they describe the different textures of the leaves? Which of the flowers are scented? Are old roses or new roses the most scented? How would they describe these scents? Are there plants with aromatic leaves? Can one of these leaves be crushed and passed around between members of the party? How many edible plants are there in the garden? (Careful supervision is absolutely essential here, many plants are far from edible!) All such sensations will greatly increase the creativity of the children's own writing on return to school.

Activities

Writing: Write a poem or a piece of prose describing a garden or tell a story about a garden.

Art: Draw and paint a picture of a garden.

Practical work: Make a garden in miniature (see model-making chapter, pages 26-27).

SUGGESTED PROJECT 5: THE KITCHEN GARDEN

Research

Does any of the kitchen garden of the great house remain? Was it walled–if so why? Are any of the plants that grew when the kitchen garden was in full use still to be seen in the area? What did the kitchen garden produce? How many of these plants can you grow at home? Do you have your own kitchen garden and how much food does it provide in the course of the year? Are there any herbs growing in the garden? Which of these herbs were used simply for cooking and which were thought to have medicinal properties? Can you grow any of these herbs on the window sill of your kitchen at home? Do you know how each should be used?

How many of the vegetables growing in the garden had to be eaten as soon as they were ready, and how many could be stored in some way to help the family through the winter? How was this food stored before the advent of refrigerators, canning, deep freeze, de-hydration, etc.?

Activities

Writing: You have found a kitchen garden which has become disused. You would like to start it up again, perhaps to grow vegetables for the market. Write to the owner of the house with a proposition. Give full details of what vegetables you would grow, with a timetable to show sowing times, growing period and harvest. Costs, labour, fuel, etc., should be considered.

Art: Make a detailed plan of the kitchen garden redesigned as a market garden.

Practical work: Grow some vegetable plants for seed. Test them for fertility.

The Park and Estate

Chapter Five

Many historic houses still retain the land which was the basis of their original prosperity. Produce from the home farm and rents from tenant farmers formed a significant proportion of the wealth needed to maintain the great house. Many owned enough land for a proportion to be set aside as a park for the cultivation of splendid trees and to support a herd of deer. There are not many left. For teachers taking children to houses with estates, there is ample scope for project work which could not be found so neatly 'packaged' elsewhere.

SUGGESTED PROJECT 1: THE HOUSE AND ITS LANDSCAPE

Research

Which came first, the house or the landscape? How did the land come into the ownership of the family? What is known of its previous history? Why do you think the house was sited in its present position? Was it for security or is it conveniently situated for access from the main communications route? Did it grow up in association with the village, or did the village grow up round it, or divorced from it? Was it orientated to face the sun or to receive the sun on the more private rooms at the back of the house overlooking the gardens? Is it built of local materials or were the materials imported?

Activities

Written work: Write a guide for visitors to the house. Use the headings of the research section above as paragraph headings for the guide.

Art: Draw illustrations and maps for the guide and a design for the cover.

SUGGESTED PROJECT 2: THE ESTATE AS A COMMUNITY

Research

The aim here is to investigate the proposition that large country houses and their estates often operated as far as possible as independent units. This project can be greatly enriched by reference to the archives of the house, to the local parish records, and to the county records office. It can include land use analysis and a survey of the village, both at present and as shown in censuses from the previous years. Using all these sources is it possible to assess the answers to some of the following questions: When were both house and family at the height of their power and influence? How far could the estate be self-supporting in terms of food? What crops were grown and what type of crop is notable by its absence? Do the records show any ways in which such deficiencies were overcome? What trades would such an estate need to have within its boundaries? Did the estate have its own blacksmith, cooper, wheelwright, stone masons and builders, etc.? In addition to farming, was there an adequate supply of timber from the woodlands? Was fishing available? Was hunting a major activity? Some items must inevitably be imported into any estate; for example, where did it get its salt from? Which local town developed as the main market and centre for local trade? Where else were major purchases made?

Activities

Writing: Having decided the period when the house and family were at the height of their prosperity and power, write a guide for visitors to the house at that time (it is noteworthy that most large historic houses in this country have always been open to visitors).

Art: Draw and paint scenes appropriate to the period of the guide. Design a cover for it.

Craft: Make peepshows of scenes appropriate to the guide (see model-making chapter, page 25).

SUGGESTED PROJECT 3: THE FUTURE OF THE LANDSCAPE

Research

Can pupils discover what recent changes there have been in the landscape? Has the village increased in size, and if so, have the new houses been tastefully built? Do they fit in with the rest of the architecture? Or are they totally unsympathetic? Have they been provided by the owner, private capital investment, or local authority spending? Have the woodlands on the estate grown or been reduced in size? Are they being maintained or are they overgrown and straggly? Have any roads been improved or widened? Are there plans for any changes of this nature in future? Has the appearance of the outside of the house received as much attention as the interior? Which do you imagine will have priority in future? How has the farmland changed and how will it change? Have hedgerows been extracted, and if so, is this process continuing? Are different crops or varieties of stock now kept than were kept in, say, the middle of the nineteenth century or slightly earlier? Why do you think such changes in farming may have occurred?

Activities

There is scope here for older children to write a properly organised thesis with appropriate plans and photographs. A report with recommendations would be a good way of presenting the work.

SUGGESTED PROJECT 4: TREES AND FORESTERS

Research

If there is woodland available on the estate then there is a great variety of texts which suggest practical work for schools in the area of woodland ecology. The area less often covered is that of forestry and the uses of our woodlands. It is very useful for children to meet foresters as they are one of the only groups of people in the present day who are planning 90-150 years ahead. The study of forest produce can be very rewarding. What sort of trees are grown, why are they grown, how is the timber used, is it used locally or sold for use elsewhere? Which is the best timber for furniture making, house building, for use in mines or shore defence, etc.?

What forest crafts are carried on on the estate, or were carried on there until recently? Are there such people as hurdle makers, broom makers, and so on, living in retirement in the area? Which trees on the estate are grown for amenity? When were they planted and why? Is there an active policy for the renewal of woodland or is it simply being harvested at present?

Activities

A serious study based upon one or several visits to an estate could involve a group of, say, twenty children with the subject sub-divided into: trees for timber; forest crafts; forest planning; forests and wildlife.

Chapter Six

Models for Projects

In the following pages, examples are given of how waste materials can be used to make models to support projects based upon historic houses. All the techniques shown have been successfully used in schools and, indeed, form part of a course of lectures given by the author to many teachers' centres, colleges of education and individual schools. It is not suggested that the completed models illustrated will themselves be suitable for any projects decided upon by teachers, but the techniques in general could be useful, adapted as necessary.

TOOLS AND MATERIALS

The techniques suggested are designed for use in the classroom as opposed to the craft room and consequently only very simple tools are needed. The following tools and materials should be sufficient for all purposes: craft knives (Swann Morton with straight blades are recommended), scissors, sticky tape (one dispenser per classroom is a help), Newclay, Plasticine, oil-based crayons, corrugated paper, powder paints, compasses and dividers, rulers, strawboard or thick card or hardboard for bases to the models.

Washing-up liquid is a wetting agent. Use it, added to water for powder paint to make the paint adhere to greasy surfaces such as cream cartons. Also use it to speed up the process of soaking newspaper to make *papier mache*. Old telephone directories make good pads for gluing and painting—tear out the soiled page and there's a clean one underneath.

SAFETY PRECAUTIONS

Most waste materials, by virtue of their use in the home, are absolutely safe for use as craft materials. The following precautions, however, should be observed:

1. When cutting open empty detergent packets make sure that any residue of powder left inside is carefully brushed away. Some children's hands are sensitive to detergent in concentrated form.
2. Do not use containers which have held corrosive materials such as ammonia or caustic soda.
3. Do not sandpaper polystyrene, the dust can be harmful. Plastic meat and fruit trays come into this category.
4. Always use craft knives with sharp blades—it is the blunt blade, pressed hard to make it cut, which slips and injures.

BUILDINGS

Empty detergent packets make excellent basic structures for the representation of buildings. Either make the roof trusses of packets cut diagonally (1) or they can be made from plastic meat trays (2). Cover the packets with corrugated or plain paper (2) or paint them with a thick paste of Polyfilla (3). Windows can be made from sections cut from plastic meat trays. Use a tool such as the blade of a screwdriver to mark the window panes (4), or cut window panes from black or grey gummed paper and stick them down leaving white frames.

1

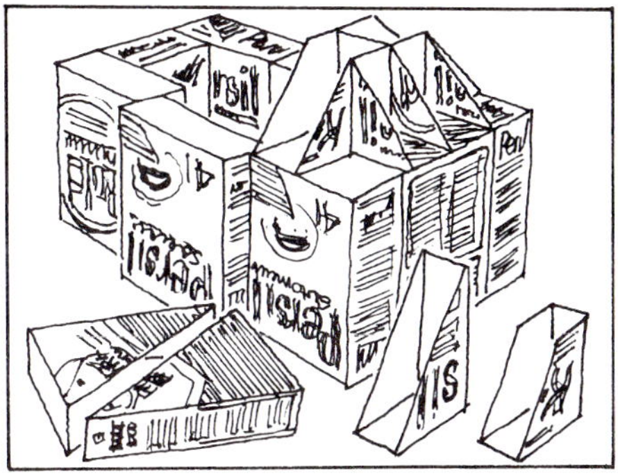

2

3

4

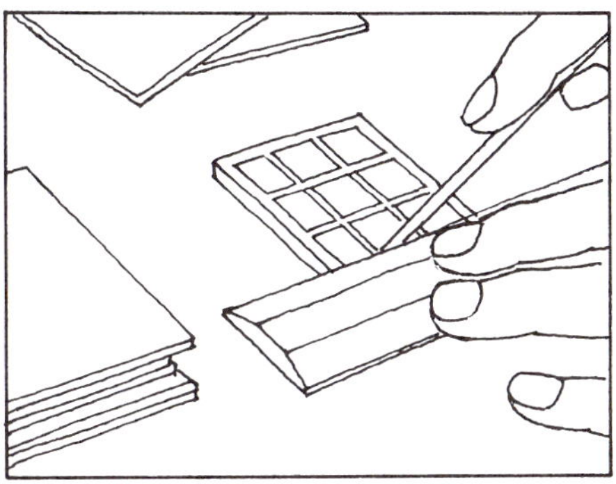

If plastic meat trays have been used for windows, colour them with a wax crayon (5). Corrugated paper makes an excellent roof if the corrugations are all folded down or flattened in the same direction and scored across to simulate tiles or slates (6). Parapets, mouldings, gables, etc., made from meat trays and strips of card are glued on (7). Finally, windows and doors are glued on (8).

5

6

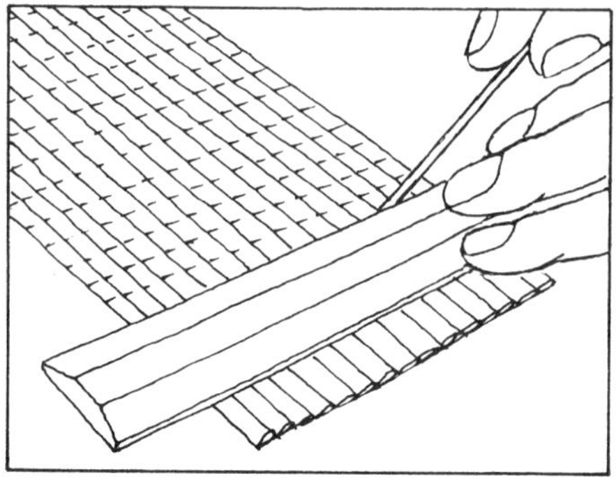

7

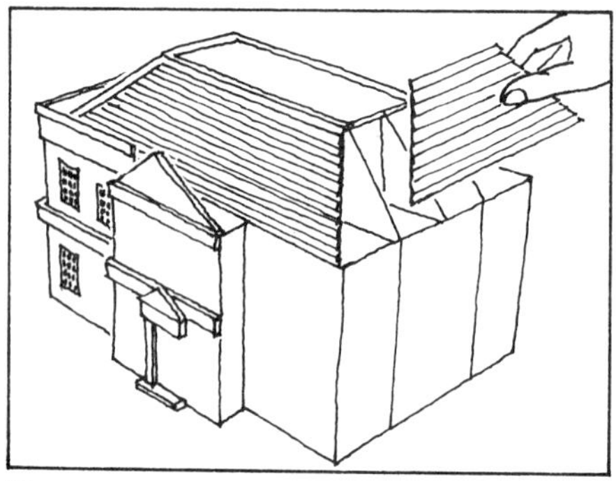

8

PEEPSHOWS

Very effective models can be made inside large cartons. They are cut open first for working purposes (note the square hole cut in the lid) and a card is cut to fit the base, arrowed (1). The scene can either be built on the base card or direct into the peepshow box (2).

Matchsticks, meat trays, Plasticine and card can be used to make furniture. Paint it in the right colours. Picture postcards of paintings from houses can be used on the walls–make frames from card or meat trays and paint them with gold paint. Panelling and plaster mouldings or decoration can be made and stuck to the walls. Painted ceilings or decoration can be painted flat on paper and then pasted down on to the model. Chandeliers can be made from florist's wire, fuse wire and small glass or plastic beads (3). When the scene is finished, the lid of the carton is closed down. A sheet of corrugated paper is fixed over the front and a peephole cut. The square hole in the lid will let in enough light. Cover it with tracing paper (4).

1

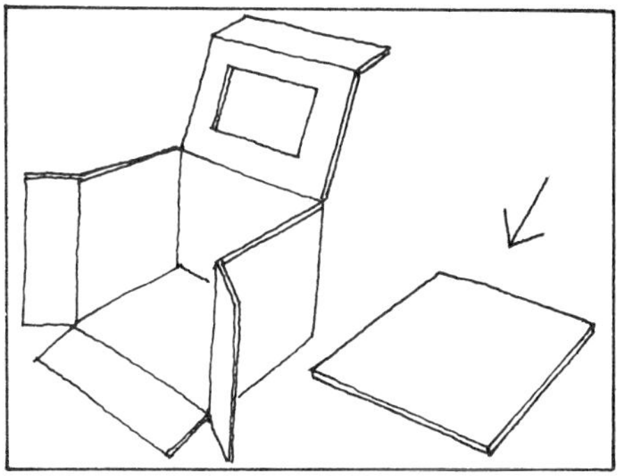

2

3

4

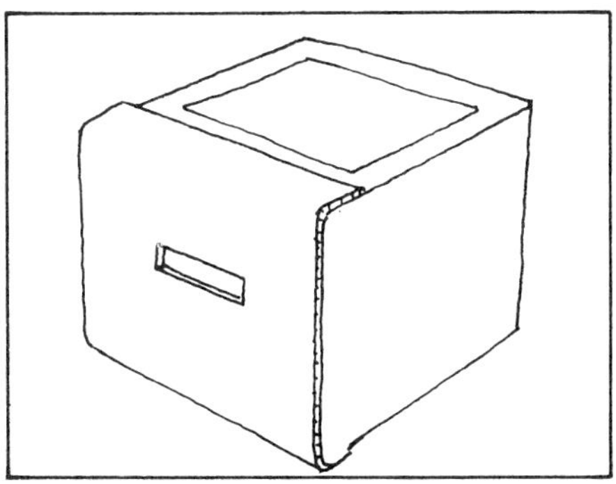

LANDSCAPES AND GARDENS

The shape of the landscape is formed from packets on a base which are completely covered with a sheet of polythene–a plastic dust sheet is best (1). Newspapers are soaked in water (washing-up liquid added speeds the process) and the surplus water squeezed out. They are then opened out and laid on top of the polythene (2). Newclay is plastered on to the wet paper where vegetation is to grow and dry powder paint is sprinkled on to the wet newspaper and scrubbed in with a stiff brush (3). Moss and rock plants are planted in the clay and rocks, cliffs, paths, etc., are painted in (4).

1

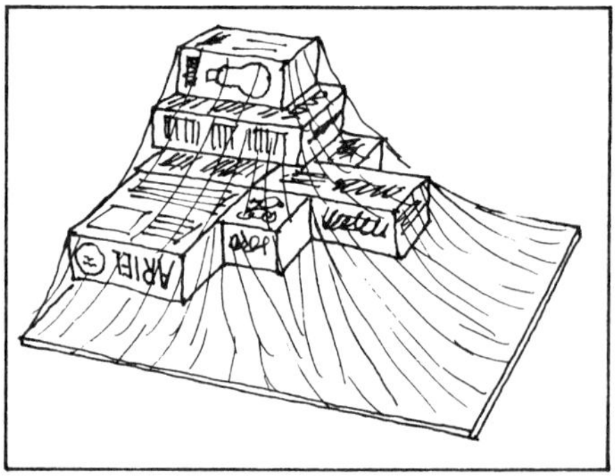

2

3

4

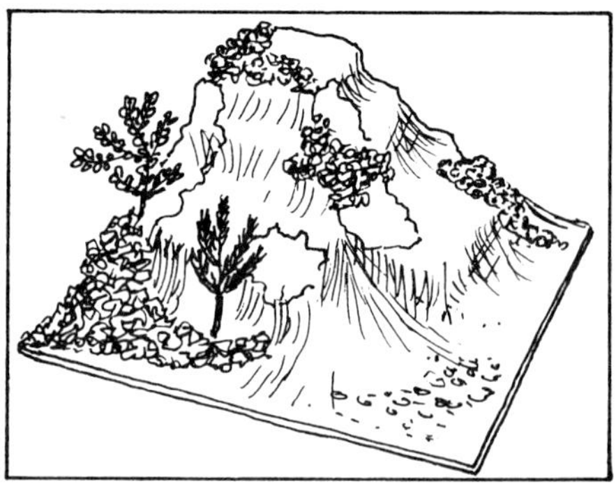

Gardens can be made by the same method using pebbles for rockeries and sections cut from plastic meat trays for crazy or regular paving. Meat trays will hold water and so make good ponds (5).

Small branches cut from shrubs make trees; moss and rock plants provide flower beds. The lawns are made from powder paint scattered on the wet clay as before (6).

5

6

VEHICLES

Wheels can be made in two ways: Detergent bottle tops for hubs with cocktail sticks as spokes. Plasticine makes the felloes and a rim cut from a plastic carton top makes the tyre. The axle is half-inch dowelling (1). The hub can also be made from a strip cut from a plastic meat tray rolled up and kept rolled with double-sided sticky tape. The felloes are rings cut from the same plastic tray. Both rings are edged with double sided sticky tape and fitted to the spokes like this (2).

A coach body can be cut from two detergent packets or one 'giant' size one (3).

Springs are best made from rings cut from washing-up liquid bottles of two different sizes so that one will fit into the other (4).

1

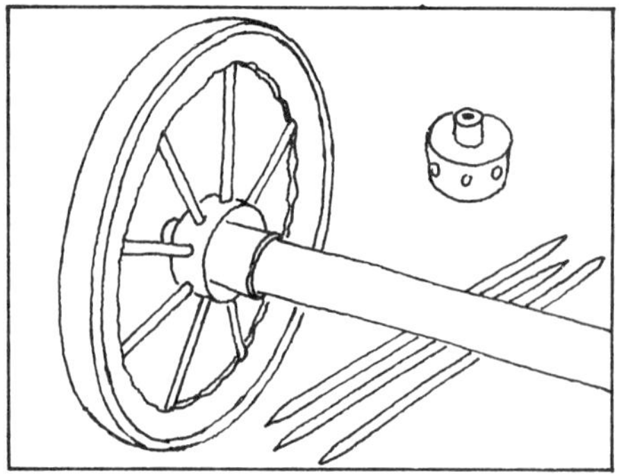

2

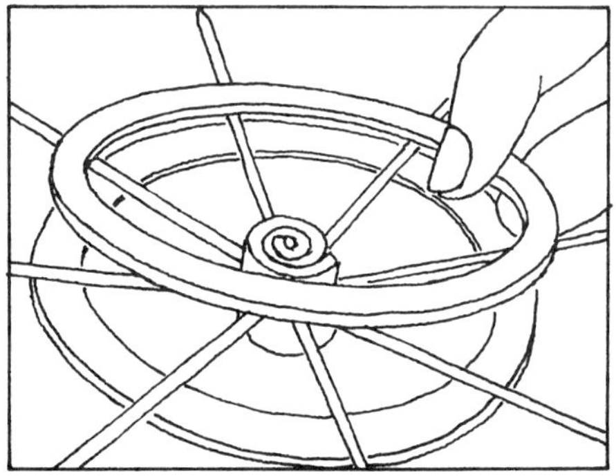

3

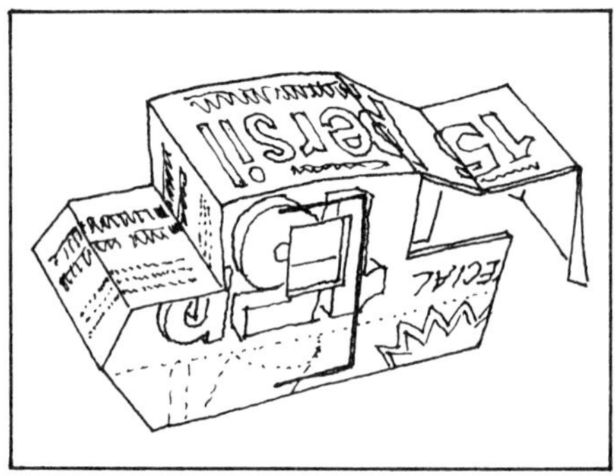

4

Squash the springs into an oval shape (5). The springs are fitted to the bottom of the coach body (6), and when fitted to the axles the body can be painted to look most realistic (7). Seats, etc., are made from sections cut from plastic meat trays.

5

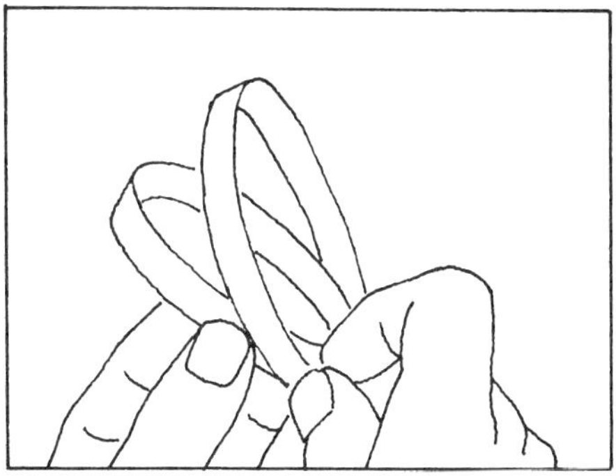

6

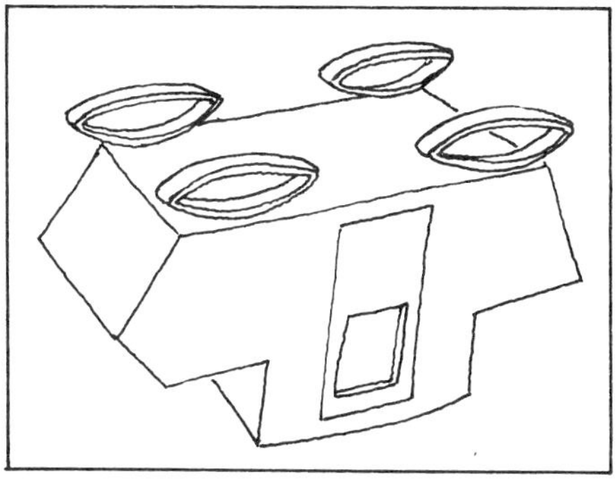

7

Chapter Seven

Checklist and References

CHECKLIST

1. Find out what children can collect without damage: leaves, cones, lambswool from fences, etc.
2. Take plastic bags and jam jars for collecting.
3. Clip boards or plastic covered wallets for worksheets.
4. Take school film camera, tape recorders, 'instamatics,' especially if you are on a school journey or you want to collect a lot of material to work on when you return to the classroom.
5. Encourage children to take pocket money to spend on sweets, apples, etc. But plan with them in advance a scheme to buy postcards, etc., for their projects.
6. Find out where lavatories are, litter bins, a place to eat sandwiches if it is wet.
7. Some houses actually have adventure playgrounds; find out from owners in any case where children can run free and adventurously. Identify any danger spots.
8. Tell the house you are coming, check times of opening and avoid crowded days, etc.
9. Inform village cafe to expect you and that you will be doing village survey, etc. Tell them which school you are, find out where drinking water is available.
10. Take additional equipment for bark rubbing (cobblers wax) and sugar paper, etc., magnifying glasses for looking at insects in rotten wood or pond dipping, and binoculars. A good idea is to climb to the nearest high landmark; this adds to the adventure and uses up physical energy—looking around helps the sense of place. Plan questions for worksheets, e.g. why is the house within a hundred yards of the river?—answer, within long bow shot, etc.
11. Creative written work: lots of ballads and songs of famous families and lovely ladies. Children can write their own.
12. If your visit goes successfully and you are a nearby school, you may like to build up more worksheets, creative teaching ideas, nature collections, taped interviews, etc. Let the house-owner know you have adopted him and his family. Write a 'thank you' letter after each visit.
13. If you have a long bus journey to return to school, ask the children to make up, with a partner, one question for a quiz on the house. This will tell you what has really interested them and you can use the quiz in preparing for your next visit.
14. Assembly/parent evening. A school occasion could be built round your trip. It would consolidate the learning experience and give children a chance to communicate their enthusiasm to others. If your school is not too far from the historic house, the owner or custodian would almost certainly enjoy an invitation to the occasion.

REFERENCES

Techniques for the model-making sections of each suggested project in the preceding chapters are fully covered, using waste materials, in the following books by Harry Sutton:

For children to use in the classroom
History Workshop—People and Their Homes: *Long Long Ago* (ISBN 304 93507 7); *Into Roman Times* (ISBN 304 93510 7); *The Invaded Isle* (ISBN 304 93597 2); *Into Tudor Times* (ISBN 304 93598 0); *100 Years of Change* (ISBN 304 93614 6); *Into Modern Times* (ISBN 304 93622 7)
From Cassell & Collier Macmillan Publishers Limited, 35 Red Lion Square, London WC1R 4SG, 80p each (less the usual discounts for schools).

For Teachers
Teaching with Models: This is a reference book which sets out a large number of practical techniques available to teachers without any experience of craftwork which simplify the making of models from waste materials. Each technique is explained, stage by stage, in a series of photographs accompanied by a brief text. Contents: General Principles; Models for Project Work; Problem Solving; Organisation in the Classroom; Buildings; Ships and Boats; Vehicles; Landscapes and Seascapes; Working Models; References and Index. (ISBN 237 29121 5)
From Evans Brothers, Montague House, Russell Square, London WC1B 5BX. Hardback, illustrated throughout in black and white, £3.95.

Harry Sutton has also written a new series of books for the National Trust called 'The Inside Story' series. The first four titles are: *Honest Rogues: The Inside Story of Smuggling; Long-Distance Flyers: The Inside Story of Bird Migration; Ride a Cock Horse: The Inside Story of the Stagecoach;* and *For King or Commons: The Inside Story of Roundheads and Cavaliers.* Each book has three chapters: the first a carefully researched story, the second a factual account of the background; the third a chapter relating the subject to places cared for by the National Trust.
From Heritage Books, 86 Brancaster Lane, Purley, Surrey. Profusely illustrated in black and white and colour, 48 pages, limp covers, 80p each.

Information
Special arrangements are made by the Department of the Environment for free admission of school parties to the many historic monuments in their care. Application forms for free admission can be obtained by writing to the Department of the Environment at:
In England: AMB/P, 25 Savile Row, (Room G1), London W1X 2BT.
In Scotland: Sec.S3, Room J 708, Argyle House, 3 Lady Lawson Street, Edinburgh EH3 9SD.
In Wales: Ancient Monuments Administration, Phase 1, Ty-Glas, Llanishen, Cardiff CF4 5UP.

Education Officers
Two education officers have been appointed by the Department of the Environment to whom reference may be made as follows: General matters concerned with school visits to historic monuments (other than specific arrangements for free entrance as above): Miss Alison Heath, 25 Savile

Row, (Room G1), London W1X 2BT. Matters concerning school visits to HM Tower of London: Mr P. T. Hammond, Education Officer, HM Tower of London, London EC3.

Addresses of National Trust Regional Information officers

Devon and Cornwall: Saltram, Plympton, Devon PL7 3UH. Tel. (0752) 336492.

East Anglia (Norfolk, Suffolk, Cambridgeshire): Blickling, Norwich NR11 6NF. Tel. Aylsham (026 373) 3471.

East Midlands (Derbyshire, Nottinghamshire, Lincolnshire, Leicestershire, Northamptonshire, parts of Staffordshire, Cheshire and South Yorkshire): Clumber Park, Worksop, Notts. S80 3BE. Tel. Worksop (0909) 3509.

Kent and East Sussex: The Estate Office, Scotney Castle, Lamberhurst, Tunbridge Wells.

Northern Home Counties (Buckinghamshire, Bedfordshire, Hertfordshire, Essex, parts of Oxfordshire and Berkshire, Greater London north of the Thames): Hughenden Manor, High Wycombe, Bucks HP14 4LA. Tel. High Wycombe (0494) 28051.

Northumbria (Northumberland, Durham, Tyne and Wear): Scots' Gap, Morpeth, Northumberland NE61 4EG. Tel. Scots' Gap (067 074) 234 and 601.

North West (Cumbria, Lancashire): Broadlands, Borrans Road, Ambleside, Cumbria LA22 0EJ. Tel. Ambleside (096 63) 3003.

Severn (Hereford and Worcester, Gloucestershire, most of Warwickshire, West Midlands): 34-36 Church Street, Tewkesbury, Glos. GL20 5SN.

South Midlands (most of Berkshire, Oxfordshire and Hampshire, the Isle of Wight, part of Warwickshire): 22 London Street, Faringdon, Oxfordshire SN7 7AD. Tel. Faringdon (0367) 20371.

Surrey and West Sussex (includes Greater London south of the Thames and parts of Hampshire): Polesden Lacey, Dorking, Surrey RH5 6BD. Tel. Bookham (0372) 53401.

Wessex (Avon, Dorset, Somerset, Wiltshire): Stourton, Warminster, Wilts BA12 6QD. Tel. Bourton, Dorset (074 784) 224.

West Midlands (Cheshire, Merseyside, Salop, most of Staffordshire, Greater Manchester): Attingham Park, Shrewsbury, Salop SY4 4TP. Tel. Upton Magna (074 377) 202 and 659.

Yorkshire (includes Cleveland, Humberside, North, South and West Yorkshire): 32 Goodramgate, York YO1 2LG. Tel. York (0904) 29621.

Northern Ireland: Rowallane House, Saintfield, Ballynahinch, Co Down BT24 4LH. Tel. Saintfield (0238) 510721.

North Wales (Clwyd, Gwnedd, part of Powys): Dinas, Betws-y-Coed, Gwynedd, LL24 0HG.

South Wales (Gwent, West Glamorgan, Mid Glamorgan, South Glamorgan, Dyfed, part of Powys): 22 Alan Road, Llandeilo, Dyfed SA19 6HU. Tel. Llandeilo (055 82) 3476.

The National Trust for Scotland, 5 Charlotte Square, Edinburgh EH2 4DU.